The saddest thing to me in looking back on my life, has been to recall, not so much the wickedness I have been involved in, the cruel and selfish and egoistic things I have done, the hurt I have inflicted on those I loved - although all that's painful enough. What hurts most is the preference I have so often shown for what is inferior, tenth-rate, when the first-rate was there for the having. Like a man who goes shopping, and comes back with cardboard shoes when he might have had leather, with dried fruit when he might have had fresh, with processed cheese when he might have had cheddar, with paper flowers when the primroses were out

-Malcolm Muggeridge

You learn a few things as you go along and one of them is that the world breaks everyone and afterward many are strong at the broken places. Those that it does not break it kills. It kills the very good and the very gentle and the very brave impartially. If you are none of these you can be sure it will kill you too but there will be no special hurry.

-Ernest Hemingway

Six Paths to a Good Life

Max Malikow

Six Paths to a Good Life

Library of Congress Control Number: 2018951089

ISBN 9780998560694

To Wendy Armenta: Whose head and heart make her an exceptional physician and friend.

To Frank Binder: Whose good life ended on September 10, 2017.

To Mark Karper: Who went to the brink and returned to us.

Acknowledgment

The "ripple effect" (also known as "the butterfly effect") theorizes every event has effects emanating well beyond itself. In the spring of 2004 Susan Scharoun, Associate Professor of Psychology at LeMoyne College, recommended to Sam Gorovitz, Director of the Renee Crown Honors Program of Syracuse University, that he consider me for a teaching position. At the end of the current semester (Spring, 2018) I will have completed 14 years on the Renee Crown faculty. This book is one of several influenced by my work at Syracuse University.

I acknowledge and thank Dr. Scharoun for thinking of me and enough of me to have made a recommendation that enriched my career well beyond anything I imagined it could be. I am the beneficiary of the ripple effect of her thoughtfulness.

Preface

Irvin Yalom, an existential psychiatrist and prolific author, maintains all psychotherapy is reducible to two questions: (1) What do you really want? and, (2) Is your current lifestyle conducive to what you really want? (1989, pp. 3-4). Implicit in his analysis is the possibility that patients will discover they do not really want what they claim is most important to them or they will have to change their lifestyle to accommodate to their strongest desire. Thirty years of practice as a psychotherapist compels me to agree with Dr. Yalom. Hence, this book on the pursuit of a good life.

Every book I have written was written for a specific audience. This one was written for patients and clients who are seeking their path to a good life. Often, they do not immediately realize this is why they have entered into counseling or psychotherapy. Just as a clothier cannot offer a one-size-fits-all garment neither can I provide the one path everyone must follow to arrive at a good life. This brief treatise describes six approaches to life that are time-tested and worthy of consideration.

To a degree, but certainly not entirely, life is a solitary journey for each of us. Friedrich Nietzsche realized this and wrote:

No one can build you the bridge on which you, and only you, must cross the river of life. There may be countless trails and bridges and demigods who would gladly carry you across; but only at the price of pawning and forgoing yourself. There is one path in the world that none can walk but you. Where does it lead? Don't ask, walk! (2018).

Max Malikow
Syracuse, NY
March 27, 2018

Table of Contents

Introduction

Happiness is not simply the absence of despair. It is an affirmative state in which our lives have both meaning and pleasure.

-Gordon Livingston

If happiness is understood as a joyous state of being then this book is not about happiness. Eudaimonia, the Greek word often translated as "happiness," more accurately means "the flourishing life." (This is what Aristotle had in mind when he spoke of happiness.) In the King James Bible, Proverbs 3:13 reads, "Happy is the man that findeth wisdom, and the man that gettith understanding." The Hebrew word translated as "happy" (esher) more accurately means "supremely fortunate." The same is found in the New Testament where Jesus concludes a lesson to his disciples with, "If ye know these things, happy are ye if ye do them" (John 13:17). Here the Greek word translated as "happy" (markarios) more accurately means "fortunate."

William James defined happiness as "persistent enjoyment" and although he believed uninterrupted pleasure was unattainable he considered it the ultimate motivation for human activity:

> If we were to ask the question, "What is human life's chief concern?" one of the answers we should receive

would be: "It is happiness." How to gain, how to keep, how to recover happiness is in fact for most men the secret motive for all they do, and of all they are willing to endure (1902, p. 77).

This belief has intellectual appeal since happiness is rarely, if ever, spoken of as an intermediate goal. Consider statements like, "When I graduate, then I'll be happy," or "When I get a good job, then I'll be happy," or "When I fall in love, then I'll be happy." Happiness is nearly always spoken of as the destination rather than a means to an end because it is the end. A sentence that begins with, "When I'm happy, then ..." is virtually never heard.

However, a well-known thought experiment devised by Hilary Putnam, a philosopher and mathematician, implies happiness is not the ultimate motivation. His "brain in a vat" thought experiment was intended to disprove the belief that objects in the world exist independently of how they are perceived and everything seen or heard is untethered to reality.

If that were the case, Professor Putnam argued, then a human brain would be no different from a brain in a vat placed there by a mad scientist. Human brains, however, employ words based on the things they refer to, which requires some kind of contact with those things. So the brain in a vat - call him Oscar – could not formulate the sentence "I am a brain in a vat," because Oscar has no experience of a real brain or a real vat. Rather, he would actually be saying something like "I'm the image of a brain in the image of a vat" (Weber, 2016).

If this thought experiment is applied to the question of happiness as the ultimate motivation, how would most people respond to the opportunity to have their brains removed, placed in a vat, and stimulated to experience uninterrupted pleasure? Would they choose continuous, disembodied happiness over a real life occasionally punctuated by happiness? At least some people would reject this opportunity, thereby demonstrating happiness is not the ultimate motivation. (This hypothetical has been presented to dozens of my students over the years and nearly all of them said they would opt for the real life.)

The renowned psychologist Henry Murray believed human behavior always makes sense because all actions are attempts to satisfy one or more of 27 "psychogenic needs" (1938). One of these needs is "sentience" - the need to experience sensual pleasure. Another is "play" - the need to relieve tension, have fun or relax. These two needs could be understood as the pursuit of enjoyment, but several of the other 25 have no relationship with uninterrupted pleasure (e.g. achievement, autonomy, nurturance, order, and recognition.) To accomplish, be independent, help others, organize, and gain approval often require diligence and sacrifice.

This book is not about happiness as "persistent pleasure" but happiness as "overall life contentment." As stated in its title, it is concerned with a good life and how to attain it. (Of course, this will require defining a good life.) Psychiatrist Gordon Livingston believes it takes nearly a lifetime to learn how to live a good life, making the pursuit of a good life a frustrating endeavor. In *Too Soon Old, Too Late Smart* he explains the reason for this frustration with a story from his days as an army officer:

> Once a long time ago, I was a young lieutenant in the 82nd Airborne Division, trying to orient myself on a field problem at Fort Bragg, North Carolina. As I stood studying a map, a platoon sergeant, a veteran of many junior officers, approached. "You figure out where we are, lieutenant?" he asked. "Well, the map says there should be a hill over there, but I don't see it," I replied. "Sir," he said, "if the map don't agree with the ground, then the map is wrong." Even at the time, I knew I had just heard a profound truth.
>
> Over the years I have spent listening to people's stories, especially all the ways in which things can go awry, I have learned that our passage through life consists of an effort to get the maps in our heads to conform to the ground on which we walk. Ideally, this process takes place as we grow. Our parents teach us, primarily by example, what they have learned.
>
> Unfortunately, we are seldom wholly receptive to these lessons. And often, our parent's lives suggest to us that they have little useful to convey, so that much

of what we know comes to us through the frequently painful process of trial and error (2008, pp. 1-2).

This trial and error process is observable in the Hebrew Bible's Book of Ecclesiastes. The author, King Solomon according to rabbinic tradition, describes his life in terms of numerous failed attempts at securing contentment. The declaration that life is meaningless provides a refrain for the book:

> I denied myself nothing my eyes desired; I refused my heart no pleasure. My heart took delight in all my work, and this was the reward for all my labor. Yet when I surveyed all that my hands had done and what I had toiled to achieve, everything was meaningless, a chasing after the wind, nothing was gained under the sun (New International Version, 1:10-11).

> ... The wise man has his eyes in his head, while the fool walks in the darkness; but I came to realize the same fate overtakes them both. Then I thought in my heart, the fate of the fool will overtake me also. What then do I gain from being wise? I said in my heart, "This too is meaningless." For the wise man, like the fool, will not be remembered; in days to come both will be forgotten. Like the fool, the wise man too must die (2:14-16).

Introduction

After characterizing life as a trial-and-error exercise in which numerous paths to a good life are tried and found wanting, the author concludes the book on a somewhat less dour note:

> Now all has been heard; here is the conclusion of the matter: Fear God and keep his commandments, for this is the whole duty of man (12:13).

A psychologists who has weighed in on the subject of a good life is Erik Erikson. His Psychosocial Theory of Development proposes eight stages of life, each of which has a crisis calling for resolution. The last stage, reached in the few remaining years of life, he labeled "integrity versus despair." At this stage people reflect on their life and feel either a sense of satisfaction (integrity) or failure (despair). This appraisal can be made only by the individual who has lived the life under review. (This concept is revisited in chapter VII: Can a Life Be Wasted?)

I. Happiness

Consider your origins, you were not made to live as brutes but to follow virtue and knowledge.

-Dante Alighieri

Action may not bring happiness but there is no happiness without action.

-William James

Early in the *Nichomachean Ethics* Aristotle provides a formula for happiness with his oft quoted definition: "Happiness proves to be activity of the soul in accord with virtue" (1999, 1098a.15). Terrance Irwin, in his translation of the *Nichomeachean Ethics*, posits to translate *eudaimonia* as "happiness" is misleading if happiness is identified with pleasure: "If Aristotle understood it this way, the question of what happiness is would hardly be puzzling" (p. 333).

What Aristotle had in mind when he spoke of happiness was "a good life," which he believed resulted from personally meaningful activity and adherence to a moral code over a lifetime. He taught that a good life requires making choices, some of which may be difficult because of the frequent temptations to settle for easier tasks and immediate gratification. Adding to the difficulty is the paradox that good character is required to resist these temptations but it is only by resisting them that good character is built. Finally, since

I. Happiness

"one swallow does not make a spring" neither are episodes of meaningful activity and virtuous conduct sufficient for a good life (1098a.20). The characteristics of a good life are not intermittent; they are developed over many years and become consistent, if not unfailing.

Meaningful Activity

When Sigmund Freud was asked what a normal person should be expected to do well, he is reputed to have responded, "work and love" (Erikson, 1963, p. 265). Even if Freud did not say this, Leo Tolstoy did when he wrote, "One can live magnificently in this world, if one knows how to work and how to love, to work for the person one loves and love one's work" (Troyat, 1967, p. 158).

A simple calculation shows why meaningful work is important. Thirty-five years of employment consists of 70,000 hours at work, which is approximately ten percent of the hours lived in an 80 year life. Framed in this way, if one hour of boredom is unappealing consider the impact of 70,000 hours of ennui. Steve Jobs, the illustrious entrepreneur and inventor, alluded to boredom in his 2005 commencement address at Stanford University. (He had been diagnosed with pancreatic cancer two years earlier and succumbed to it in 2011.)

> (F)or the past 33 years, I have looked in the mirror and asked myself: If today were the last day of my life, would I want to do what I'm about to do today?" And

whenever the answer has been "No" for too many days in a row, I know I need to change something (2005).

In *Flow: The Psychology of Optimal Experience* Mihalyi Csickszentmihalyi theorizes people are happiest when they are in a state of complete absorption in an activity in which nothing but the activity matters (1990). He labeled this state of optimal intrinsic motivation *flow*, in which there is a loss of self-awareness and a loss of the sense of the passing of time.

Love

Meaningful activity is necessary, but insufficient, for a good life. Love and moral excellence are also required. Concerning love, Erikson named the sixth stage of psychosocial development "intimacy versus isolation." According to his theory, starting in adolescence, individuals develop the capacity for intimate love. A failure to develop this capability results in loneliness and social isolation. A study of the daily experiences of American teenagers shows they self-reported being unhappy when alone and happiest when with friends (Csikszentmihalyi and Hunter, 2003).

Moral Excellence

Concerning moral excellence, the power of guilt to eradicate contentment is eloquently expressed in Nathaniel Hawthorne's classic, *The Scarlet Letter*. Set in Puritan New

I. Happiness

England, it is the story of a woman whose extramarital affair resulted in an illegitimate child and the public scorn that went with adultery. The woman, Hester Prynne, carried herself with dignity, raised her child, and never disclosed the identity of her lover. Her lover was Reverend Dimmesdale, the community's respected spiritual leader. He lived out his years maintaining his image as a man of God. His inauthentic life, known only to him and Hester, is given this description by Hawthorne:

> It is the unspeakable misery of a life so false as his, that it steals the pith and substance out of whatever realities there are around us, and were meant by Heaven to be the spirit's joy and nutriment. To the untrue man, the whole universe is false - it is impalpable - it shrinks to nothing within his grasp. And he himself, in so far as he shows himself in a false light, becomes a shadow, or, indeed, ceases to exist (1978, p. 107).

Dimmesdale also fits the description of the Roman playwright Plautus when he wrote, "Nothing is more wretched than the mind of a man conscious of guilt" (2017).

II. Stoicism

There is only one way to happiness and that is to cease worrying about things which are beyond the power of our will.

-Epictetus

In common parlance a stoic is a person who is calm and not excitable, bearing difficulties or discomfort without complaint, and apparently indifferent to pleasure or pain. The term derives from a school of philosophy that flourished for over half a millennium, from the 3rd century B.C. to the 3rd century A.D. Its founder, Zeno of Cittium, and followers taught the path to eudaimonia is accepting each moment as it presents itself without wishing it were otherwise and without being controlled by the desire for pleasure or fear of pain. This requires asking in every circumstance, "Can I control or, at least, influence this situation?"

The foundation of Stoicism is the belief that reason is superior to emotion in the management of life. Reason derives from logic, and logic will unfailingly direct individuals toward what they ought to do. Emotion is an unreliable guide and will lead people away from what they should do. Of course, this raises the question of how to determine what ought to be done in a given situation. The answer offered by Stoicism is there is a natural order in the universe to which people are called to live in accord. Since nature is logical in its operation, it is logic, rather than emotion, that will provide individuals with the path to overall life contentment. This idea is reminiscent of William James' definition of religion as "the attempt to live in harmony with an unseen order of things" (1901, Lecture III).

A literary example of an individual required to make a decision in which emotion and reason are in conflict is Francesca Johnson in Robert James Waller's novel, *The Bridges of Madison County*. Published in 1992, it had a run of almost 150 weeks on the *New York Times'* bestseller list (38 weeks as number one) and surpassed *Gone with the Wind* as the all-time bestselling hardcover fiction book. The story begins in the late summer of 1965 when Robert Kincaid stopped at an Iowa farm house to ask directions. There he encountered Francesca Johnson, alone at home while her husband and two children were visiting the Illinois State Fair. Kincaid, a 52-year-old photographer on assignment for *National Geographic*, was seeking the location of seven covered bridges for a photo shoot. As he approached the middle-aged woman on the front porch he saw that, "She was lovely, or had been at one time, or could be again" (Waller, 1992, p. 16). With this encounter began a four-day romance, "an erotic, bittersweet tale of lingering memories and forsaken possibilities" (*Publishers Weekly*, 2006, p. 2).

Waller makes no attempt through his characters to justify their adultery; his elegant prose describes and explains their passion without defending their behavior. On the eve of the return of Francesca's husband and children she refuses Kincaid's offer to leave with him while admitting to her lackluster life:

Yes, it's boring in a way. My life, that is. It lacks romance, eroticism, dancing in the kitchen candlelight, and the wonderful feel of a man who knows how to love a woman. Most of all, it lacks you. But there's this damn sense of responsibility I have. To Richard, to the children. Just my leaving, taking away my physical presence, would be hard enough for Richard. That alone might destroy him…as much as I want you and want to be with you and part of you, I can't tear myself away from the realness of my responsibilities (Waller, 1992, pp. 115-116).

Francesca reasoned if she left her family she would take with her the memory of her responsibilities and awareness of the pain she had caused: "If I did leave now, those thoughts would turn me into something other than the woman you have come to love" (p. 116). Had her decision been determined by emotion she would have abandoned her family for a life with Kincaid. Logic forced upon her the conclusion that such indulgence would transform her into a person she did not want to be.

A real-life application of stoical logic is the story of Vice Admiral James Bond Stockdale, a prisoner of war in North Vietnam for seven and one-half years (four years in solitary confinement). After his release he was awarded the Congressional Medal of Honor, appointed President of the United States Naval War College, and served as President of The Citadel, the Military College of South Carolina. Stockdale credits his survival as a POW to the teaching of the Stoic philosopher Epictetus. After parachuting from his disabled Skyhawk fighter and "drifting along in a silence interrupted only by the whizz of bullets that luckily passed by me only to tear holes in the parachute canopy above me" Stockdale said to himself, "You are leaving the world of technology and entering the world of Epictetus" (Bennett, 1993, p. 517). Over the next nearly eight years these words of Epictetus sustained Stockdale:

> There are things which are within your power, and there are things which are beyond your power. Within your power are opinion, aim, desire, aversion; in a word, whatever affairs are your own. Beyond your power are body, property, reputation, office; in a word, affairs not properly your own. Concern yourself only with what is within your power.
>
> The essence of good consists of things within your own power; with them there is no room for envy or emulation. For your part, do not desire to be a general, or a senator or a consul, but to be free; and the only way to do this is a disregard of things which do not lie within your power (p. 517).

The value of classifying situations as either within or outside of an individual's power was popularized by Daniel Goleman in his bestseller, *Emotional Intelligence* (1995). Emotionally intelligent people are able to identify, understand, manage, and use emotions to think creatively in order to solve problems and adapt to situations. During his captivity Stockdale kept hope separate from expectation. He maintained hope that he would one day be liberated but did not expect it to happen soon or on any specific day:

> I never lost faith in the end of the story, I never doubted not only that I would get out, but also that I would prevail in the end and turn the experience into the defining event of my life, which, in retrospect, I would not trade (Doherty, 2018 p. 1).

When asked why some did not survive the POW experience he said,

> Oh, that's easy, the optimists. Oh, they were the ones who said, "We're going to be out by Christmas." And Christmas would come, and Christmas would go. Then they'd say, "We're going to be out by Easter." And Easter would come, and Easter would go. And then Thanksgiving, and then it would be Christmas again. And they died of a broken heart (p.1).

This distinction between hope and expectation has been referred to as the "Stockdale Paradox," a phrase coined by Jim Collins, the author of *Good to Great*, to describe one of the six characteristics of "good" businesses that become "great" (2001). These businesses confront brutal facts without losing faith in eventual success. Collins acquired this concept from his interview of Stockdale in which Stockdale said,

> This is a very important lesson. You must never confuse faith that you will prevail in the end - which you can never afford to lose - with the discipline to confront the most brutal facts of your current reality, whatever they might be (2018, p.1).

Hope directs individuals to address the world as they would like it to be, expectation directs them to confront the world as it is, including its harsh realities.

III. Hedonism

Nature has placed mankind under the governance of two sovereign masters, pain, and pleasure. It is for them alone to point out what we ought to do, as well as to determine what we shall do.

-Jeremy Bentham

Perhaps it is because the philosophy known as hedonism derives its name from the Greek word for "pleasure" (*hedone*) that it is widely misunderstood. The popular misconception of a hedonist is an individual who pursues sensual pleasure, however transitory, in an unbridled manner, regardless of consequences. A cursory reading of Epicurus' writings is sufficient to dispel this misunderstanding. (Epicurus is widely considered a spokesman for hedonism.) Hedonists strive to maximize pleasure and minimize pain, thus making life as enjoyable as possible. However, as already stated, this does not mean casting aside morality and responsibility at every opportunity for pleasure. Instead, it means carefully considering which actions will contribute to happiness over a lifetime. Epicurus addressed this in his *Letter to Menoceus*:

> When therefore, we maintain that pleasure is the end, we do not mean the pleasures of profligates and those that consist in sensuality, as is supposed by some who are either ignorant or disagree with us or do not

understand, but freedom from pain in the body and from trouble in the mind. For it is not continuous drinkings and revellings, nor the satisfaction of lusts, nor the enjoyment of fish and other luxuries of the wealthy table, which produce a pleasant life, but sober reasoning, searching out the motives for all choice and avoidance, and banishing mere opinions, to which are due the greatest disturbance of the spirit (Bowie, Michaels, Solomon, 2007, p. 565).

Epicurus taught the purpose of philosophy is to instruct on how to pursue a life of tranquility and freedom from fear (Greek: *ataraxia*) and an absence of pain (Greek: *aphonia*). He believed people who are highly self-sufficient and surrounded by friends and have achieved *ataraxia* and *aphonia* have all that is needed for a good life. The philosophy that bears Epicurus' name (Epicureanism) and hedonism are not identical schools of thought but sufficiently similar for the terms to be used interchangeably. Both philosophies discourage indiscriminate pleasure seeking since many short-term pleasures have unpleasant long-term consequences:

... we do not choose every pleasure, but sometimes we pass over many pleasures, when greater discomfort accrues to us as the result of them: and similarly we think many pains better than pleasures, since a greater pleasure comes to us when we have endured pains for a long time (p. 565).

The counsel of both schools is a good life consists of pleasures that have been considered in the light of their long-term disadvantages and pains in the light of their long-term advantages. Epicurus described these calculations to his friend Menoceus:

> Yet by a scale of comparison and by the consideration of advantages and disadvantages we must form our judgment on all these matters. For the good on some occasions we treat as bad, and conversely the bad as good (p. 565).

A contemporary expression of this idea was provided by the legendary hockey player Wayne Gretsky when he said, "You always miss 100 percent of the shots you don't take" (2018). Although technically an unattempted shot is not a missed shot, he made the point that shooting and missing provides the same result as not taking a shot. "The Love Song of J. Alfred Prufrock" is a poetic example of a man who did not take a shot. A drama of literary anguish, it tells the story of a man afraid to risk rejection by declaring his love for the woman he admires from afar. The protagonist, Prufrock, is self-conscious about his physical imperfections that include a bald spot and spindly arms and legs. Hence, he vacillates about making his feelings known to her:

> Do I dare
> Disturb the universe?

III. Hedonism

In a minute there is time
For decisions and revisions which a minute will
reverse ...

Should I, after tea and cakes and ices,
Have the strength to force the moment to its crisis?
But though I have wept and fasted, wept and prayed,
Though I have seen my head (grown slightly bald)
brought in upon a platter,
I am no prophet - and here's no great matter,
I have seen the moment of my greatness flicker,
And I have seen the eternal Footman hold my coat, and
snicker,
And, in short, I was afraid.
(Eliot, 1920).

Prufrock never declares his love, leaving him alone at the
end of his life to wonder about the life he might have had:

I grow old ... I grow old ...
I shall wear the bottoms of my trousers rolled.

Shall I part my hair behind? Do I dare to eat a peach?
I shall wear white flannel trousers and walk along the
beach.
I have heard the mermaids singing each to each.

I do not think that they will sing to me (1920).

In contrast, Alfred Lord Tennyson wrote:

> 'Tis better to have loved and lost
> Than to have never loved at all (1850).

Prufrock loved and lost - his loss resulting from inaction. He weighed risk against reward and determined the risk was not worth the reward. He miscalculated the pain of rejection would be greater than the pain of wondering what might have been.

IV. Altruism

Every man must decide whether he will walk in the light of creative altruism or in the darkness of destructive selfishness.

-Rev. Dr. Martin Luther King, Jr.

Altruism is innate but it's not instinctual. Everybody's wired for it, but a switch has to be flipped.

-David Rakoff

Altruism is unselfish devotion to the welfare of others. Theologian David Elton Trueblood vigorously advocated for altruism when he wrote, "A man has made at least a start on discovering the true meaning of human life when he plants shade trees under which he knows full well he will never sit (1951, p. 58). Philosopher and novelist Ayn Rand, who is featured in the next chapter, expressed strenuous disagreement with Trueblood when she wrote, "If any civilization is to survive, it is the morality of altruism that men have to reject" (2018).

The Greater Good Science Center at the University of California at Berkeley promotes altruism, citing studies that indicate it contributes to personal well-being "emotionally, physically, romantically, and perhaps even financially" (2018). Psychologist Sonja Lyubomirsky, author of *The How of Happiness*, believes altruism enriches relationships because, "Being kind and generous leads you to perceive others more positively and charitably" (2008, p. 130). The implication of such claims is altruistic acts are contaminated by self-interest. Thomas Hobbes believed this and argued that people perform good deeds to feel good about themselves rather than to help others, rendering altruism an impossibility. Thomas Katen is among those who disagree with Hobbes, seeing his argument as mere semantics:

> To discover if there are altruists is not a matter of playing with definitions but of finding if there are individuals out there who fulfill the requirements of the definition. What we have to do is discover if there are instances of behavior in which individuals actually consider the well-being of others before their own and do not have any ulterior motives that we can empirically demonstrate. What Hobbes and others claim is that there is always an ulterior motive. But if we cannot specifically find it, do we have the right to simply assume it is there, as Hobbes does? (1973, p. 234).

Even if someone admitted to self-satisfaction from an action on behalf of someone else, this would not disqualify it as altruistic. That good feeling might be an unintended consequence of the action rather than the motivation for it. Moreover, it is not a requirement of altruism that the individual feels miserable for the unselfish act. Finally, even if undiluted altruism is an impossibility, it would not preclude selfless acts as a path to a good life.

Just as Mother Teresa served a generation of baby-boomers as a paradigm of self-sacrificial human service, Albert Schweitzer did the same for the previous generation. The son of a Lutheran pastor, he distinguished himself throughout Europe as a musician and theological scholar by age 28. In 1896 he reflected on what he considered his life of privilege and made a decision about his future.

> One brilliant summer morning at Gunsbach, during the Whitsuntide holidays - it was in 1896 - as I awoke, the thought came to me that I must not accept this good fortune as a matter of course, but must give something in return. ... What the character of my future activities would be was not yet clear to me. I left it to chance to guide me. Only one thing was certain, that it must be direct human service, however inconspicuous its sphere (Schweitzer, 1933, p. 82).

"From everyone who has been given much, much will be demanded; and from the one who has been entrusted with much, much more will be asked" (Luke 12:48, New International Version). With these words Jesus commissioned his disciples. Schweitzer's gratitude for what he had received accounts for his resolution to spend the balance of his life giving. After committing himself to hands-on human service he became aware of the need for a physician in equatorial

Africa. Upon learning of this need, he entered medical school at the University of Strasbourg in 1905 and graduated in 1912. He explained his determination to serve as a physician in terms of its contrast to his life as a scholar: "I wanted to be a doctor that I might be able to work without having to talk because for years I have been giving myself out in words" (1933, p. 82).

Had Sigmund Freud been aware of Schweitzer's altruistic intention he would have questioned Schweitzer's rationale for his unselfish devotion to human service. In *Civilization and Its Discontents* Freud postulated indiscriminate love is of little worth:

> ... readiness for a universal love of mankind and the world represents the highest standpoint which man can reach. ... I should like to bring forward my two main objections to this view. A love that does not discriminate seems to me to forfeit a part of its own value, by doing an injustice to its own object; and secondly, not all men are worthy of love (1989, p. 66).

Rand, perhaps altruism's most vehement critic, would question the value Schweitzer placed on his own life and if he respected those he served:

> If a man accepts the ethics of altruism, he suffers the following consequences (in proportion to the degree of his acceptance): (1) Lack of self-esteem - since his first

concern in the realm of values is not how to live his life, but how to sacrifice it. (2) Lack of respect for others - since he regards mankind as a herd of doomed beggars crying for someone's help (1961, p. 49).

A less renowned but equally impressive example of altruism is Albert Lexie. He has donated over $220,000 to the Free Care Fund of Children's Hospital in Pittsburgh, Pennsylvania. While this amount is impressive, what makes it amazing is that he earned only $10,000 a year shining shoes. The $220,000 came from the tips he accumulated over 35 years before retiring in 2017. The Free Care Fund is for children whose families cannot afford their medical care. A beloved figure at the hospital, he has been recognized by several organizations for his philanthropy and featured in several stories, including a biography, *Albert's Kids: The Heroic Work of Shining Shoes for Sick Children* (Rouvalis and Maurer, 2012).

Andrea Jaeger also fulfills the requirements of the definition of altruism. In 1981, at the age of 16, she was the second ranked women's professional tennis player in the world. Six years later she retired from tennis and moved to Aspen, Colorado with $1.4 million she had won on the tour and founded the Little Star Foundation, devoted to programs for seriously ill, abused or at-risk children. In 2006 she made another significant life change when she became Sister Andrea, an Anglican Dominican nun.

IV. Altruism

Often she has been asked if she misses tennis and thinks about the career she might have had if she had not retired at 23. "No regrets," has been her response, "God wanted me to do something else, and it happened to be helping children with cancer. I love what I do" (Bane, 2006). She is reminiscent of the Christian martyr Jim Eliot who wrote, "No man is a fool who gives up what he cannot keep to gain that which he cannot lose" (2017).

The philosopher Thomas Nagel has written, "Altruism itself depends on a recognition of the reality of other persons, and on the equivalent capacity to regard oneself as merely one individual among many" (1970, p. 100). This is precisely what Charles Dickens' character, Jacob Marley, failed to recognize during his earthly walk. In his post-mortem visitation to Ebenezer Scrooge the condemned Marley urges Scrooge to take heed of the suffering around him and respond to it benevolently:

> Mankind was my business. The common good was my business. ... I walked through crowds of my fellow creatures with my eyes downwards. If but my eyes had been led to see the misery around me, which was in my power to remove. But like yours Scrooge, these eyes saw nothing (2011, p. 16).

Nagel believes altruism results when people recognize the things they want for themselves are the same things every person desires. In contrast to Rand, Nagel does not believe altruistic acts are expressions of a lack of self-esteem on the part of the giver and condescending view of the recipient. He believes altruism is generated by the recognition that everyone is entitled to certain goods and the world works better when as many people as possible have them.

V. Egoism

Nobody does anything for the good of others; but as he pursues his own interests, he is brought to work unwittingly for the benefit of the many.

-Bangambiki Habyarimana

Egoism can be spoken of psychologically or ethically. The former addresses what egoism is; the latter addresses whether it ought to be. Psychological egoism claims personal welfare is the ultimate aim of everyone. Ethical egoism claims an action is morally right if it maximizes the actor's self-interest. Ayn Rand advocated ethical egoism and denounced altruism in *The Virtue of Selfishness*:

> Altruism declares that any action taken for the benefit of others is good, and any action taken for one's own benefit is evil. Thus the beneficiary of an action is the only criterion of a moral value - and so long as that beneficiary is anybody other than oneself, anything goes (1961, p. viii).

She justified the characterization of selfishness as a virtue by distinguishing the popular usage of the word selfishness from its dictionary definition.

V. Egoism

In popular usage, the word "selfishness" is a synonym for evil; the image it conjures up is of a murderous brute who tramples over piles of corpses to achieve his own ends, who cares for no living being and pursues nothing but the gratification of the mindless whims of any immediate moment.

Yet the exact meaning and dictionary definition of the word "selfishness" is: concern with one's own interests.

This concept does not include a moral evaluation; it does not tell us whether concern with one's own interests is good or evil; nor does it tell us what constitutes man's actual interests. It is the task of ethics to answer such questions (p. vii).

Rand's contemptuous view of altruism includes the assertion that it is a form of suicide since altruists sacrifice their life to serve the interests of others. But this does not mean she encouraged the indulgence of any and every whim:

Morality is not a contest of whims. ... Just as man cannot survive by any random means ... so man's self-interest cannot be determined by blind desires or random whims, but must be discovered and achieved by the guidance of rational principles" (p. xi).

She understood that actions motivated by immediate gratification are likely to be counter-productive to long-term self-interest. Recall Francesca, the character in *The Bridges of Madison County* referred to in chapter II. She refused to run away with Kincaid because the pain this would cause her family would make her miserable and unhappy in the long run.

Another criticism of altruists is they are enablers who actually harm the people they intend to help. Although enabler is not a technical psychological term, it is widely understood as someone who facilitates another person's self-destructive behavior. By providing means and excuses for the behavior enablers perpetuate a problem, often preempting the natural consequences of a maladaptive behavior. Ironically, enablers often harm the people they intend to help by doing things for them they can and should be doing for themselves.

According to Rand, selfish people, as she defined them, pursue their best interests without depriving or enabling others. Believing people should earn what they get and get only what they earn she wrote, "human good does not require human sacrifices and cannot be achieved by the sacrifice of anyone to anyone" (p. 34). For Rand, since anything unearned is undeserved, human relationships should be based on the principle of trade in which each person is a trader:

> A trader does not expect to be paid for his defaults, only for his achievements. He does not switch to others the burden of his failures, and he does not mortgage his life into bondage to the failures of others (p. 35).

V. Egoism

Integral to her philosophy is "there is no conflict of interests among men who do not desire the unearned" (p. 34).

Aristotle's Principle of the Golden Mean teaches a virtue is the apex between two diametrically opposed extremes. Applying this principle to the accumulation and distribution of wealth, one extreme is wanton extravagance in which the welfare of others is a matter of indifference. The other extreme is total divestiture of wealth and distribution to those in need. An example of this is found in the New Testament where Jesus directs a wealthy man to, "Sell everything you have and give to the poor, and you will have treasure in heaven" (Luke 18:22).

The apex between these extremes is exemplified by Andrew Carnegie, the Scottish-American industrialist who amassed great wealth and then donated $350,000,000 to various causes in the last 18 years of his life. The "Andrew Carnegie Dictum" proposed a man should spend the first third of his life acquiring an education; the next third making as much money as possible, and the last third giving it all away to worthy causes. (Of course, to follow this dictum literally a man would have to know exactly how long he would live.) Carnegie died in 1919 at the age of 83, but not before he had donated 90 percent of his fortune to causes he deemed worthy. He believed a man who dies wealthy dies in disgrace. In his essay, *Wealth*, (later titled *The Gospel of Wealth*) he wrote:

This, then, is held to be the duty of the man of wealth: First, to set an example of modest, unostentatious living, shunning display or extravagance; to provide moderately for the legitimate wants of those dependent upon him; and after doing so to consider all surplus revenues which come to him simply as trust funds, which he is called upon to administer, and strictly bound as a matter of duty to administer in the manner which, in his judgment, is best calculated to produce the most beneficial results for the community--the man of wealth thus becoming the mere agent and trustee for his poorer brethren, bringing to their service his superior wisdom, experience and ability to administer, doing for them better than they would or could do for themselves (1889).

Although a church attender, Carnegie's involvement in organized religion was minimal. However, his commitment to charitable giving was consistent with biblical teaching. In the New Testament in Paul's Letter to the Philippians he offered this balanced instruction: "Each of you should look not only to your own interests, but also to the interests of others" (2:4, New International Version). In the Old Testament the people of Israel were instructed to allow for gleaning after a harvest:

When you reap the harvest of your land, do not reap the very edges of your field or gather the gleanings of your harvest. Do not go over your vineyard a second time or pick up the grapes that have fallen. Leave them for the poor and the alien. I am the Lord your God (Leviticus 19: 9,10, New International Version).

While these biblical teachings are not consistent with Rand's assertion that anything unearned is undeserved they are compatible with her working definition of selfishness: "concern with one's own interest" as well as Carnegie's understanding of stewardship (Rand, 1961, p. vii).

VI. Buddhism

Life is available only in the present moment. If you abandon the present moment you cannot live the moments of your daily life deeply.

-Thich Nhat Hanh

The ability to be in the present moment is a major component of mental wellness.

-Abraham Maslow

The social psychologist Jonathan Haidt values the reflections of ancient philosophers as well as the results of modern psychological research. (*Finding Modern Truth in Ancient Wisdom* is the subtitle of his book, *The Happiness Hypothesis*.) He believes,

> By drawing on wisdom that is balanced - ancient and new, Eastern and Western, even liberal and conservative - we can choose directions in life that will lead to satisfaction, happiness, and a sense of meaning. ... (B)y drawing on humanities greatest ideas and best science, we can ... know our possibilities as well as our limits, and live wisely (2006, p. 243).

This collaboration of the old and new is evident when comparing a teaching of Buddhism with the modern psychological technique known as mindfulness. In both Buddhism and psychology, mindfulness is moment to moment awareness of present experience. The following anecdote provides an illustration of mindfulness from a little girl who diluted a pleasurable experience by looking to the future. (This story is written in the first person because it recounts an actual experience I had several years ago.)

> On a hot summer day in North Carolina, I stopped at an ice cream stand and got in line to be served. In front of me a little girl and her mother had just placed their order. When the girl received her ice cream cone, before taking the first lick, she asked her mother, "Mommy, when I finish this can I have another?"

I can't recall what the mother said because the girl's question immediately sent me to thinking about the first three of Buddhism's Four Noble Truths:

1. Life is suffering.
2. Suffering comes from desire.
3. Cease desiring to cease suffering.

The Buddha (Siddhartha Gautama) taught suffering derives from attachment to things and experiences that are impermanent. The desire for something pleasurable to be unending not only causes suffering but attenuates the enjoyment of the present experience. This desire must be eradicated if suffering is to cease. The girl in the story anticipated the near future when her ice cream would be finished, thereby depriving her of the full pleasure of the ice cream cone in her hand.

Of course, in a sense, every experience is in the present. The past is the present recollection of the bygone; the future is the present anticipation of things to come. What the Buddha cautioned against was misusing the present with unproductive reflections on the past or fruitless anticipatory thoughts about the future. The attractiveness of reliving past pleasures and achievements is understandable. Regretting mistakes made and recalling pains caused by others are unavoidable human behaviors. Also understandable is looking forward to a future delight and planning ahead is what responsible people do. But extended and purposeless excursions into the past or future provide no benefit. Ironically, they produce the opposite of the peaceful state of mind being sought. Sue Chance, a psychiatrist, challenges her patients to break from the past without dismissing its significance. For example, she gives the following lecture to adolescent patients who were poorly parented:

> You want to tell me how much your parents have messed up and how much pain they've caused you. I believe you. I know that your complaints are legitimate. But you're coming closer and closer to the time in your life when you can take over and make it better for yourself. That's going to be your choice:

whether you stay stuck in blaming and moaning about all the things which have been unfair or get on with it and do the best you can with what you have (1992, p. 146).

Concerning this lecture, she confesses:

> Kids don't like that message any better than adults do, any better than I did the first time I gave it to myself. But it has the utility of being true and ultimately helpful.
>
> I do not like my parents and I do not like the things they did to me. However, I am responsible for who I am now. There is no way I can reasonably say that, at forty-nine, I am more a product of the first fifteen years I spent with them than I am of the past thirty-fours years spent with myself. I would, in fact, be very ashamed of myself if it were true (pp. 146-147).

Much of what passes for planning is actually anxiety producing obsessing. The most famous of Jesus' sermons, the Sermon on the Mount, includes the instruction, " ... do not worry about tomorrow, for tomorrow will worry about itself. Each day has enough trouble of its own" (Matthew 6:34, New International Version). Since "each day has enough trouble of its own" it is imprudent to direct attention to troubles that do not exist, many of which never will. While it is true that almost anything is possible it is also true that all possible things are not equally probable.

It is also imprudent to occupy too much of the present ruminating over the past. While revisiting the past as part of planning for the future can be productive, there is no benefit to be derived from reviewing the past merely for the sake of reminiscing or assigning blame. Sir Winston Churchill understood this and said, "If we open a quarrel between the past and present, we shall find that we have lost the future" (2018).

VII. Can a Life Be Wasted?

A clean house is a sign of a wasted life.

-Anonymous

The issue of a "wasted life" is directly addressed in the movie, "Good Will Hunting" (1997). The protagonist, Will Hunting, is an off-the-chart genius with unlimited intellectual interests. Yet, he chooses to work as a construction laborer and hang out with his less cerebral friends, mostly in bars in South Boston. Eventually, his best friend challenges him to stop wasting his life, positing Will's extraordinary intellect requires him to do something more than swing a sledge hammer by day and drink beer by night.

Is it possible for a life to be wasted? Was Will Hunting wasting his life because he was working construction and not utilizing his extraordinary intelligence at more cerebral work? If so, does it follow that 6'9" tall bestselling author Michael Crichton should have played basketball instead of writing? Is a person with an exceptional attribute or capability obligated to employ it? If so, from where does this obligation originate? The phrase "God-given ability" has no influence on an atheist or agnostic. Whether a life can be wasted is an ethical issue because it implies there are right and wrong ways for spending a life. Perhaps Crichton should be excused for not playing basketball since he pursued a career as a writer and was hugely successful. (His book sales have exceeded 150,000,000 copies.) He also graduated from Harvard Medical School without ever practicing medicine. Did he have an obligation to work as a physician? Was his decision to be a writer in any sense closer to right than Will Hunting's to be a construction worker?

The possibility of a wasted life requires comparing the worth of possible lives. Waste occurs when something is used for other than its intended purpose. In addition, something can be considered wasted when it serves an inferior purpose or, even worse, a meaningless cause. In a drought people are urged not to waste water by washing cars or watering lawns. When a family's breadwinner is unemployed money is in short supply and not to be wasted on luxuries. A problem arises when presuming to speak of a life as wasted. Who determines how anyone's life ought to be used? On what basis can one person declare to another that she is wasting her life?

Curious is that each of us enters this world through no choice of our own, yet are told we are responsible for doing something meaningful with our life. Antinatalists believe no such responsibility exists; they insist it would be better to have never been born. David Benatar has written extensively on this subject in *Better Never to Have Been: The Harm of Coming into Existence* (2008). (This is not to say he advocates suicide. While he insists no life is worth starting he concedes some lives are worth continuing.)

An essay that appeared in *Newsweek* magazine the week of Mother's Day, 2010 also addresses the issue of the worthy use of a life. The author, Julia Baird, challenged the widely held view that good mothers sacrifice their careers to devote themselves to their children. Not only does she believe that being a good mother does not require choosing maternity over the pursuit of other interests, but also believes there's nothing wrong with subordinating motherhood to those interests. She wrote favorably of Nobel laureate Doris Lessing who left two toddlers behind to pursue a career as a writer. Concerning this decision, Lessing said:

> For a long time I thought I had done a very brave thing. There is nothing more boring for an intelligent woman to spend endless amounts of time with small children. I felt I wasn't the best person to bring them up. I would have ended up an alcoholic or a frustrated intellectual like my mother (Baird, 2010).

Baird does not explicitly defend Lessing's choice to renege on motherhood. However, she does encourage women to combine career and family without feeling guilty, falsely believing they must be giving their children short shrift:

> Today women no longer need to escape their families to work or be happy - now they need to escape their own unrealistic expectations of what a good mother is. ... that impossible ideal of the perfect mother has become a tyranny... Now that we are allowed to be more than mothers, we wonder if we have the time to

be anything but mothers if we are to be truly good (2010).

The renowned social philosopher Eric Hoffer had a unique life that nearly ended by suicide at age 29. Not particularly depressed, he took stock of his life and decided not to continue in the "deadening routine of a workingman's life in the city" (1983, p. 25). A flash of insight aborted his suicide while it was in progress. He lived on to have a distinguished academic career that included ten books and numerous articles, some of them while working as a longshoreman. If he had accomplished his suicide, would his life had been wasted? If he had worked as a longshoreman without writing anything, would that had been a wasted life?

Friedrich Nietzsche believed the evaluation that a life is being wasted can be made only by the one living it:

> No one can build you the bridge on which you, and only you, must cross the river of life. There may be countless trails and bridges and demigods who would gladly carry you across; but only at the price of pawning and forgoing yourself. There is one path in the world that none can walk but you. Where does it lead? Don't ask, walk! (Hicks, 2018).

VIII. Denouement

The good life is active, contemplative, somewhat fatalistic, and selfless.

-Daniel Robinson

Few people are as qualified as Daniel Robinson to speak about the characteristics of a good life. Widely recognized as a distinguished scholar in both psychology and philosophy, he believes a good life requires participation, reflection, acceptance, and charity. Each of these requirements is considered below.

The good life is active.

Novelist and poet Dorothy Sayers offers a scathing indictment of sloth, the antithesis of activity and one of the seven deadly sins:

> It is the sin that believes in nothing, cares for nothing, seeks to know nothing, interferes with nothing, enjoys nothing, hates nothing, finds purpose in nothing, lives for nothing, and remains alive because there is nothing for which it will die (Fairlie, 1979, p. 114).

Speaking at the "Great March on Detroit" the Rev. Dr. Martin Luther King, Jr. asserted, "there are some things so dear, some things so precious, some things so eternally true, that they are worth dying for. And I submit to you that if a man has not discovered something that he will die for, he isn't fit to live" (1963). Likely there are many people who could not immediately identify something for which they would die. But this failure would not make them slothful. It is people who are indifferent to everything and have an interest in nothing who are disqualified for a good life.

As previously noted, Sigmund Freud and Leo Tolstoy believed work and love are integral to overall life contentment. Concerning work, Aristotle included it in his formula for happiness (eudaimonia). Flow, referred to in chapter I, is "total immersion in a task that is challenging yet closely matched with one's abilities" (Haidt, 2006, p. 95). In a state of flow people lose self-awareness and are nescient to the passing of time. The importance of meaningful activity for happiness is evident from the simple calculation also provided in chapter I. Recall that 35 years of employment (ages 21 to 55) consists of 70,000 hours at work (50 weeks per year times 40 hours per week). When experiencing boredom, time passes slowly. Conversely, the passing of time is imperceptible in a state of flow. The thought of spending 70,000 hours (approximately ten percent of an 80-year life) in a state of boredom underscores the influence of activity on happiness.

The good life is contemplative.

In the classic play *Inherit the Wind* one of the characters, Henry Drummond, argues there is only one quality that elevates human beings above all other living things:

> The ability to think! What other merit have we? The elephant is stronger; the horse is swifter; the mosquito is more prolific; the butterfly is more beautiful; even the simple sponge is more durable (1.2).

Aristotle believed since human beings have the unique faculty to engage in thought it indicates the best possible life for them. He reasoned just as birds fly and fish swim because that is what they are made to do, so also human beings are acting compatibly with their nature when they are thinking. He also believed the pursuit of sensual pleasure is inferior to the pursuit of wisdom, which can be acquired only through contemplation. Since wisdom is necessary for the best possible life, contemplation is the superior activity. Socrates showed his agreement with Aristotle when he declared, "The unexamined life is not worth living" (Plato, 38a5-6). This assertion, part of his self-defense at his trial, expressed his belief that the best possible life includes reflection and introspection.

The good life is somewhat fatalistic.

It is important to note Professor Robinson proposes the good life is somewhat fatalistic rather than fatalistic. To be fatalistic is to believe life is a matter of living out an unalterable script written by a supernatural power from which any attempt at deviation is futile. At the other extreme is the resolve expressed by the political activist Angela Davis when she said, "I am no longer accepting the things I cannot change. I am changing the things I cannot accept" (2018). As with most extreme positions, fatalism and Davis' determination overreach. A more moderate view of life is offered by psychologist Martin Seligman in *What You Can Change ... and What You Can't* (1993). Like Robinson, Seligman believes some life conditions and personal attributes are subject to change and others are not. (Seligman does not include changing other people against their will in his list of changeable things.)

Stoicism is the philosophical counterpart to Seligman's psychological position. James Bond Stockdale, referred to in chapter II, put stoicism to the test over nearly eight years as a POW in North Vietnam. Recall that he credited his survival of isolation, starvation, and torture to Epictetus, a first century stoic philosopher. Stockdale said he retained his mental health by directing his thoughts and energy only to those things over which he had a measure of control. While he could not control whether he would be tortured, he could choose to resist as long as possible and what information he would provide. (He usually gave meaningless information.) He could not control whether he would be fed, but he could determine if he would eat his bowl of rice all at once or make it last as long as possible.

To deploy thoughts and actions toward things unchangeable guarantees frustration. To direct attention to things changeable contributes to serenity, as suggested by theologian Reinhold Niebuhr's prayer:

> God, grant me the serenity to accept the things I cannot change,
> Courage to change the things I can,
> And wisdom to know the difference (2002, p. 735).

The good life is selfless.

Twenty-five centuries ago the Greek philosopher Heraclitus taught, "All things come into being by conflict of opposites" (2018). This is the case with attending to the needs of others. Recall Trueblood's commendable view of altruism presented in chapter IV:

> A man has made at least a start on discovering the meaning of human life when he plants shade trees under which he knows full well he will never sit (1951, p. 58).

In stark contrast is Rand's denigration of altruism, also quoted in chapter IV:

> If a man accepts the ethics of altruism, he suffers the following consequences (in proportion to the degree of

his acceptance): (1) Lack of self-esteem – since his first concern in the realm of values is not how to live his life, but how to sacrifice it. (2) Lack of respect for others - since he regards mankind as a herd of doomed beggars crying for someone's help (1961, p. 49).

Aristotle's Principle of the Golden Mean, referred to in chapter V, teaches moral excellence is an intermediate position between the extremes of excess and deficiency. Applied to charity, Trueblood and Rand represent the extremes of altruism and egoism respectively. The former believes a good life is found in serving the interests of others without recompense, reward or recognition. The latter believes a good life is found in exclusive concern with one's own interests. Although Robinson uses the word "selfless" in characterizing a good life, he believes altruists benefit from their benevolence:

> A great and exalting pleasure comes from enlarging the possibilities in the lives of others; this has to meet the fundamental objectives of the hedonistic individual. Indeed, there must be great joy and pleasure in the life of a Mother Teresa, a deep sense of satisfaction for a hero knowing that he or she has saved a life (2004, p. 8).

Moreover, his respect for Aristotle's approach to morality compels the conclusion that Robinson intends "selfless" as the mean between the extremes of unadulterated altruism and unremitting egoism. He recognizes a completely selfless life is a theoretical construct rather than a life actually lived. Citing Aristotle, Robinson has written:

> Aristotle recognizes the importance of a knowledge of what constitutes moral excellence, but he also knows the whole point of such knowledge is to permit one to act in accordance with such principles. Again, the eudaimonic life is one that is actually lived in a certain way, not one that is simply dissected philosophically and abstractly as some sort of hypothetical life (Robinson, 1989, p. 113).

The Greek mythological character Echo, as the result of a curse, lost her own voice and could speak only the last words spoken to her. Using her as a point-of-reference, psychologist Craig Malkin wrote of the healthy balance between self-interest and service to others necessary for a good life:

> At the heart of narcissism lies an ancient conundrum: how much should we love ourselves and how much should we love others? The Judaic sage and scholar Hillel the Elder summarized the dilemma this way: "If I am not for myself, who am I? And if I am only for myself, then what am I?" To remain healthy and happy, we all need a certain amount of investment in ourselves. We need a voice, a presence of our own, to

VIII. Denouement

make an impact on the world and people around us or else, like Echo, we eventually become nothing at all (2015, pp. 13-14).

References

Preface

Nietzsche, F. (2018). Recovered from https://www. goodreads.com/quotes/7625719-no-one-can-build-you-the-bridge-on-which-you-walk on 03/27/2018.

Yalom, I. (1989). *Love's executioner & other tales of psychotherapy.* New York: Basic Books, Inc., Publishers.

Introduction

James, W. (1902). *The varieties of religious experience: A study in human nature.* New York: The Modern Library. Random House.

Livingston, G. (2008). *Too soon old, too late smart: Thirty true things you need to know.* Philadelphia, PA: DeCapo press.

Murray, H. (1938). *Explorations in personality.* New York: Oxford University Press.

Weber, B. (2016). "Hilary Putnam, giant of modern philosophy, dies at 89." *New York Times.* 03/17/2016.

References

I. Happiness

Aristotle. (1999). *Nichomachean ethics.* second edition. Irwin, T. translator. Indianapolis, IN: Hackett Publishing Company.

Csikszentmihalyi, M. (1990). *Flow: The psychology of optimal experience.* New York: Harper & Row.

Csikszentmihalyi, M. & Hunter, J. (2003). "Happiness in everyday life: The uses of experience sampling". *Journal of Happiness Studies*, 4, 185-199.

Erikson, E. (1963). *Childhood and society.* (2nd edition). New York: Norton.

Hawthorne, N. (1978). *The scarlet letter.* New York: Norton.

Jobs, S. (2005). *Stanford News.* 06/12/2005.

Plautus. (2017). Recovered from http://www.brainyquote.com/topics/guilt on 12/28/2017.

Troyat, H. (1967). Tolstoy. (N. Amphoux, Translator). New York: Doubleday.

II. Stoicism

Bennett, W. (1993). *The book of virtues: A treasury of great moral stories*. New York: Simon & Schuster.

Collins, J. (2001). *Good to great: Why some companies make the leap and others don't*. New York: Harper - Collins.

Doherty, N. (2018). "The Stockdale paradox." Recovered from https://ndoherty.com/stockdale-paradox/on01/03/2018.

Goleman, D. (1995). *Emotional intelligence: Why it can matter more than iq*. New York: Bantam Books.

James, W. (1901). *The varieties of religious experience: A study in human nature*. New York: Random House: The Modern Library.

Publishers Weekly. (2006). Recovered from http://www.aazon.com/gp/product on 06/19/2006.

Waller, R. (1992). *The bridges of madison county*. New York: Warner Books.

III. Hedonism

Bowie, G., Michaels, M., and Solomon, R. (2007). *Twenty questions: An introduction to philosophy*. Third edition. Belmont, CA: Thompson Wadsworth Publishing.

Eliot, T. (1920). "The love song of J. Alfred Prufrock." Recovered from http://www.batleby.com/198/1. html on 01/08/2018.

Gretsky, W. (2018) Recovered from www.brainy quote.com/quotes/wayne_gretzky_ on 01/05/2018.

Tennyson, A. (1850). Recovered from https://www. phrases.org.uk/meanings/62650.html on 01/08/2017.

IV. Altruism

Bane, V. (2006). "Tennis star Andrea Jaeger's new life as a nun." *People Magazine*. November 18, 2006.

Dickens, C. (2011). *A christmas carol*. Charleston, SC: Createspace Publishing.

Eliot, J. (2017). Recovered from http://www.goodreads .com/quotes/2919 on September 23, 2017.

Freud, S. (1989). *Civilization and its discontents*. New York: W.W. Norton and Company.

Greater good science center. University of California, Berkeley. (2018). "What is altruism?" Recovered from greatergood.berkeley.edu on 01/10/2018.

Katen, T. (1973). *Doing philosophy.* Englewood Cliffs, NJ: Prentice-Hall, Inc.

Lyubomirsky, S. (2008). *The how of happiness: A new approach to getting the life you want.* New York: Penguin Books.

Nagel, T. (1970). *The possibility of altruism.* Princeton, NJ: Oxford University Press.

Rand, A. (2018). Recovered from http://www.brainyquote .com/topics/altruism on 01/10/2018.

_____ (1961). *The virtue of selfishness.* New York: Penguin Books.

Rouvalis, C. and Maurer, S. (2012). *Albert's kids: The heroic work of shining shoes for children.* Pittsburgh, PA: RedDog Books.

Schweitzer, A. (1933). *Out of my life and thought.* Baltimore, MD: Johns Hopkins University Press.

References

Trueblood, D. (1951). *The life we prize*. New York: Harper & Brothers Publishers.

V. Egoism

Carnegie, A. (1889). "Wealth." *North American Review*. June, 1889.

Rand, A. (1961). *The virtue of selfishness*. New York: Penguin Books.

VI. Buddhism

Chance, S. (1992). *Stronger than death: When suicide touches your life*. New York: W.W. Norton & Company.

Churchill, W. (2018). Recovered from www.dreamthisday .com/quotes - sayings/past/ on 01/30/2018.

Haidt, J. (2006). *The happiness hypothesis: Finding modern truth in ancient wisdom*. New York: Perseus Books Group.

VII. Can a Life Be Wasted?

Baird, J. (2010). "Lowering the bar: When bad mothers give us hope." Newsweek. 05/17/2010.

Benatar, D. (2006). *Better never to have been: The harm of coming into existence.* Cambridge, UK: Oxford University Press.

"Good Will Hunting." (1997). Los Angeles, CA: Mirimax Films.

Hicks, S. (2018). Recovered from www.stephenhicks.org on 02/25/2018.

Hoffer, E. (1983). *Truth imagined.* Titusville, NJ: Hopewell Publications.

VIII. Denouement

Davis, A. (2018). https://www.goodreads.com on 3/24/18.

Fairlie, H. (1979). *The seven deadly sins today.* South Bend, IN: University of Notre Dame Press.

Haidt, J. (2006). *The happiness hypothesis: Finding modern truth in ancient wisdom.* New York: Perseus Books Group.

Heraclitus. (2018). Recovered from http:www.azquotes .com>Authors>Heraclitus on 03/10/2018.

References

King, M.L. (1963). "Great March on Detroit." Speech given 06/23/1963.

Lawrence, J. and Lee, R. (1955). *Inherit the wind.*

Malkin, C. (2015). *Rethinking narcissism. The secret to recognizing and coping with narcissists.* New York: HarperCollins Publishers.

Niebuhr, R. (2002). "The serenity prayer." *Bartlett's familiar quotations. (17th edition).* New York: Little, Brown and Company.

Plato (1966). *The apology.* Translated by H.N. Fowler. Cambridge, MA: Harvard University Press.

Rand, A. (1961). *The virtue of selfishness.* New York: Penguin Books

Robinson, D. (1989). *Aristotle's psychology.* New York: Columbia University Press.

_____. (2004). *The great ideas of philosophy (2nd edition).* Chantilly, VA: The Teaching Company.

Seligman, M. (1993). *What you can change ... and what you can't: The complete guide to self-improvement (learning to accept who you are)*. San Francisco, CA: Fawcett Columbine.

Trueblood, D. (1951). *The life we prize*. New York: Harper & Brothers Publishers.

About the Author

Dr. Max Malikow is on the faculty of the Renee Crown Honors Program of Syracuse University and an Adjunct Assistant Professor of Philosophy at LeMoyne College. The author or editor of 14 previous books, he is a nationally recognized authority on suicide and practicing psychotherapist in Syracuse, New York.

CPSIA information can be obtained
at www.ICGtesting.com
Printed in the USA
LVHW05s0043030818
585836LV00011B/155/P

9 780998 560694